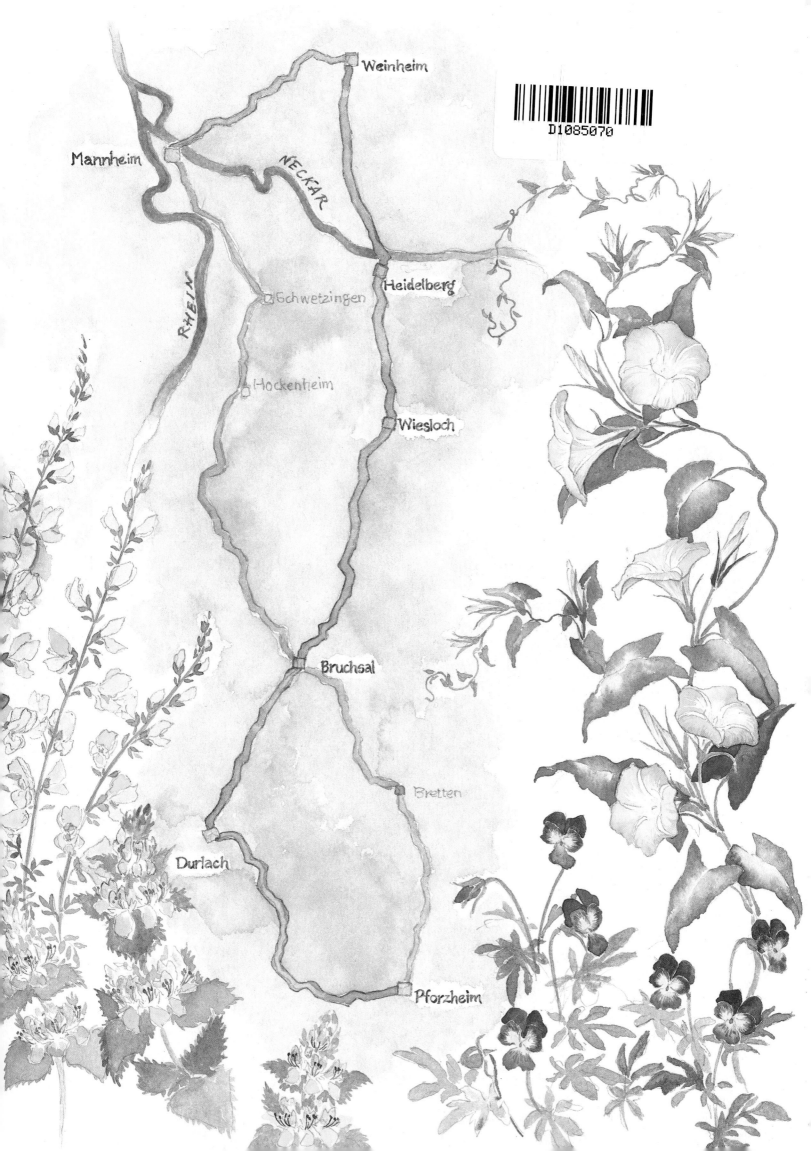

Weinheim

Mannheim

NECKAR

RHEIN

Heidelberg

Schwetzingen

Hockenheim

Wiesloch

Bruchsal

Bretten

Durlach

Pforzheim

Berta Benz and the Motorwagen

The Story of the First Automobile Journey

Written by Mindy Bingham
Illustrated by Itoko Maeno
Edited by W. Robert Nitske

Advocacy Press, Santa Barbara

*To my dad who steered me
in the right direction.*

*To my mother who taught me
to take risks.*

Text Copyright © 1989 by Melinda W. Bingham
Illustration Copyright © 1989 by Itoko Maeno

 Published by Advocacy Press
P.O. Box 236
Santa Barbara, California 93102

Advocacy Press is a division of the Girls Incorporated of Greater
Santa Barbara, an affiliate of Girls Incorporated.

**girls
inc.**

Book layout by Christine Nolt

Library of Congress Cataloging-in-Publication Data

Bingham, Mindy, 1950-
Berta Benz and the motorwagen: the story of the first automobile journey

Summary: Recounts the story of the first automobile journey, made by Berta Benz and her
two teenage sons in 1888.
  Bibliography: p.
  [1. Automobiles — Touring — History — 19th century. 2. Benz, Berta. Juvenile literature.]
I. Maeno, Itoko, ill. II. Title.
GV1021.B55   1989
796.7 — dc20   89-6867 CIP AC

ISBN 0-911655-38-7
10 9 8 7 6 5 4 3 2
Printed in Hong Kong

*Special thanks to the archive department
of Daimler-Benz Museum in Stuttgart,
West Germany and W. Robert Nitske.*

*E*s ist nicht eine Dummheit!"* Karl Benz growled under his breath as he ripped up the letter he had just finished reading.

Berta Benz, his wife, looked up from her project. She didn't need to ask what was wrong. This had become a familiar occurrence.

"That was another rejection letter," Herr Benz grumbled. "It was from a man I approached about buying one of the Motorwagens. He called it a silly toy and said it would never have any practical use."

It was more than two years since Karl Benz had driven his first three-wheeled motor carriage on the streets of Mannheim, Germany. Yet on this summer afternoon in 1888 very few people knew of the automobile's existence...and those who did usually laughed at it.

"It is not a folly."

"Karl, you have to show people that your Motorwagen can replace the horse and carriage," Berta gently reminded her husband.

"How?" he snapped back in frustration. "The Bürgermeister passed a law making me responsible for any accidents it causes. So I can only drive on the street around our house. It's no wonder the farthest I've ever driven is only one mile."

"Poor father," Richard, their younger son, sympathized as Karl stomped off in disgust.

Richard and Eugen, the Benz's two teenage sons, along with Berta were just as frustrated as Herr Benz.

"Mother's right!" Eugen added as soon as his father couldn't hear him. "Until the Motorwagen completes a cross-country journey, no one is going to take it seriously."

Berta's face brightened. "I have an idea how we can help." Lowering her voice, she added, "But we'll have to keep it a secret."

"Next week the three of us are going to visit your grandmother in Pforzheim," she confided. "That's nearly 60 miles away. Instead of taking the train, let's take one of the Motorwagens."

"Oh, Mother, that's a brilliant idea!" Richard said admiringly. Then his face darkened. "But we've never driven before."

"How hard can it be?" Eugen observed. "We have all ridden with father when he drives. We've also helped him in the shop and know how to repair the Motorwagens."

"Besides," Berta reminded them, "one of your grandmother's concerns is saving overworked horses, so your father's invention is of great interest to her. I know she would love to see it."

Berta paused and thought for a moment. Then she continued, "But I don't think your father will be as excited about our idea as we are. We'll have to come up with a strategy for borrowing the Motorwagen without his knowing it."

The three conspirators put their heads together to plan their "escape".

One week
later, the sun wasn't
even up as Berta,
Richard, and Eugen
pushed the car out of the
shed and down the street.

"Be very quiet, boys," their
mother warned. "Your father would
surely stop us if we woke him up."

About one block from the house Eugen went to the
engine in the back, turned the fly wheel and the car sputtered
into action. He then jumped into the driver's seat and adjusted the lever
on the steering column.

The engine fired up. *Chick-a-pooka, chicka-a-pooka, chick-a-pooka.*
With a soft cheer, Berta and Richard jumped on board.

Off they went…on roads not made for their horseless carriage. There
were no road maps and no service stations. They had no covering over
their heads to protect them from bad weather and because there was no
room, they had not brought any luggage.

Caught up in the excitement of the proposed journey, they hadn't
really taken the time to anticipate what lay ahead.

The first hour went by quickly. By the time the sun was peeking over the hills they had covered 14 miles. Berta kept a close eye on their inexperienced driver, Eugen.

As the little vehicle rambled down the road, people would stop and stare in amazement. A carriage without a horse? How could that be?

The three adventurers enjoyed the attention and excitement created by the car. They were in the middle of congratulating themselves on the success of their scheme when, suddenly, the engine began to smoke.

They had forgotten that the engine needed a constant supply of…

...WATER!

Because this first car had no radiator, the water that kept the engine cool boiled off and had to be replaced about every 12 miles.

The search for water was a constant concern. Luckily they were able to find it at spots along the route.

But water wasn't their only problem....

"You need how much ligroin*?" The pharmacist almost choked on his words. "Frau Benz, I can get you 2½ gallons… but it will take 10 days. All I have right now is one quart."

Berta had to laugh at herself. Shaking her head, she wondered why she had not anticipated how much fuel the car would require for such a long journey. Oh, well, she thought, they would just have to make the best of it and stop at every pharmacy they passed.

She turned to her younger son, "Richard, I saw another pharmacy down the street. Please run down and buy all the ligroin they have."

*Dry-cleaning fluid used as fuel.

By now crowds had begun to gather at each town and stop. Word raced ahead of the trio and people flocked to the roadside to admire their strange contraption.

In the city of Bruchsal, some say Berta sent a telegram to her husband.

The boys and I decided to borrow the Motorwagen rather than take the train to Pforzheim STOP All is going well STOP

Your devoted wife, Berta

The next time the car's engine sputtered to a stop, Berta hoped she had not been overconfident.

Eugen jumped down from the driver's seat and peered at the motor. After a minute of tinkering he found the problem.

"The fuel line is clogged, Mother," he said with disgust. "and we have no tools."

Berta thought for a minute and then with an infectious grin stepped out of the car to help her son. "I have just the answer," she said as she reached up and took out…

…her hat pin!

In a matter of minutes they had resumed their journey.

Hills presented another problem. The car's 3-horsepower engine and two gears couldn't pull it up an incline. Berta and Eugen had to get out and push while the steering wheel was turned over to a very excited and lightweight Richard. As they puffed uphill behind the car, Berta turned to Eugen and said, "When we get home, remind me to advise your father to add another gear and more horsepower."

As they crested the hill and started down the other side, they quickly discovered that going uphill was not nearly as bad as…

…going downhill.

SQUEEEEEEEEEEEEEK………
"Hold on tight!" Berta yelled above the screech of the brakes as the car careened down the hill.

The air filled with the smell of burning leather as the brake lining wore through.

At the bottom of the hill Richard and Berta inspected the damage.

Obviously the brakes were not designed to stop that much weight. Berta made another note to herself to talk to her husband about that problem.

"What do we do now, Mother?" Richard asked. "The leather lining on the brakes is completely worn away."

"I know just the person to help us," Berta replied.

At first the shoemaker in the next village was apprehensive about working on the strange machine. But after a quick inspection he confidently set to work to repair the brakes. Once again, Berta and the boys were back on the road in only a short time. By now it was late afternoon. With their destination within range, the trio sang folk songs as the little car chugged along the country road.

Chick-a-pooka, chick-a-pooka, chick-a-pooka.

All of a sudden they heard a loud clang. The motor rattled for a moment and then the car came to an abrupt halt.

"What now?" Richard cried as they all hopped down to look over the engine.

Eugen reached into the motor and pulled out a broken spring cable. "I think this is the end of the trip," he said gloomily.

"I wouldn't be so sure about that," said Berta undaunted.

"Where are we going to get a cable?" Richard looked skeptically at his mother. "We're out in the middle of nowhere."

Berta looked around. "I think I know just the place," she called over her shoulder as she headed into the nearby bushes.

A few minutes later she returned swinging...

…her garter belt.

"Mother, you're a genius," Eugen cried. "The rubber should be perfect."

As the sun sank behind the old castle on the hill, the three of them set to work to repair the broken cable.

Just outside Pforzheim, even though their destination was within sight, they could go no farther. Night had fallen and the car had no lights. With no street lights in the town to brighten their way, they were stopped once more.

"I guess we'll have to camp overnight here beside the Motorwagen," Berta said. "It's just too dangerous to continue."

Suddenly the sky in the distance began to glow. What started out as a speck of light grew larger and larger as it moved toward them.

What was coming down the road? The closer it came, the brighter and brighter the light grew until…

...they could see it was a parade of people carrying torches and lanterns. Word of their journey had preceded them, and the villagers had gathered to help escort this remarkable trio and their even more remarkable contraption through the dark streets.

"*Willkommen,* Frau Benz" the leader called out. "We heard of your brave adventure and thought you might need some assistance this last mile."

"*Danke,*" Berta called out. She was touched by the enthusiasm of the crowd.

What a sight the group made as they paraded through the streets of the village on the way to the hotel.

It was too late to get in touch with grandmother that evening.

But it was not too late to cable Herr Benz.

**We have arrived safely in Pforzheim STOP
We must have by return express a set of chains STOP
Your Partner, Berta**

As soon as the telegram was sent, Berta had a moment to reflect upon what they had done. Turning to Eugen and Richard, she took a deep breath and sighed, "I hope your father is not angry."

Angry? When Herr Benz received the telegram the following morning he was too proud to be angry.

"Hans," he called to his friend, "let's take a set of chains off one of the other Motorwagens. We need to get them to the train station right away."

The next day when Berta and her sons arrived at her mother's home all the neighbors were there to greet them.

As people mingled around the car, Berta raised her voice so everyone could hear.

"You see, Mother," Berta explained, "someday the Motorwagen will replace the horse and cart. A machine will do the work that an animal does today."

The crowd gasped in disbelief.

"Yes, it's true," Berta said confidently. The crowd listened thoughtfully as she explained all the practical uses of a motorized vehicle.

For five days Berta or the boys drove grand-mother throughout the neighboring towns and villages. Everywhere they went, a crowd gathered to listen to Berta talk about the future of the horseless carriage.

The vacation passed quickly and soon it was time to go home. Berta was anxious to get back and share their adventures and the results of their road test with her husband. She was also anxious to get everyone into some clean clothes. Since they hadn't been able to bring luggage, their clothes were covered with dirt and grease.

All the townspeople turned out to wish the celebrities a safe journey home.

As everyone waved good-bye and called out *"Auf Wiedersehen,"* they probably didn't realize they had just witnessed history in the making.

Because of the determination and daring of this farsighted woman, they would someday be able to tell their grandchildren, "I was there when the very first automobile in history made its first cross-country trip."

Devoted, strong-minded wives have always stood beside their husbands and helped them to succeed. Occasionally they have even moved ahead of them to insure that their endeavors would flourish and prosper. A century ago Berta Benz did just that, with an adventure that made history: the first long-distance drive in a gasoline-powered automobile. With due respect to all the inventors, it was Frau Benz who showed the world that the automobile had a practical future.

By the summer of 1888, automobiles had been experimentally operational in Germany for almost two years. Karl Benz and Gottlieb Daimler were busy with testing and developing, but their vehicles had never traveled more than a few kilometers from their workshops.

In the Benz household there was one person who realized that the automobile had to do more than just puff around the block or shuttle back and forth from the shop to a station one kilometer away. That person was Berta Benz, wife of Karl Benz for 16 years and mother of their four children.

Berta provided emotional and financial help for her husband's dream throughout their courtship and marriage. It was Berta's dowry and support that enabled the struggling Karl Benz to set up his mechanical workshop. She was the one who urged her husband to try one more time on that fateful New Year's Eve of 1879 when the engine finally came to life. Every evening after she tucked the children into bed, she could be found either in the shop or in her living room pedaling away on her sewing machine to charge the accumulator for the car's ignition.

The great day came in August 1888. (The exact date is not recorded.) The intrepid tourists—wife, sons and one Model 3—departed for Pforzheim, 59 miles away, over roads that had never carried an automobile. They planned to make the trip in one day in a three-horsepower car with solid rubber tires and no weather protection. One more problem: They had little previous driving experience.

Given the road conditions and the developmental stage of that primitive automobile, it is hard for even veteran drivers of antique cars to imagine the courage, spirit and determination required of spunky Berta. And the long-distance drive took courage in more than one way. Besides transcending technical limits, she also flouted the law. A local law permitted only short drives on the streets of specified suburbs and held Karl Benz responsible for any accidents.

Berta earned her niche in automotive history. She provided the "push" to assure the recognition and success of the invention. More than any other individual, Berta Benz was responsible for getting the automobile out of the test stage and onto the open roads.

W. Robert Nitske, *author*
The Complete Mercedes Story

"Encourage your daughters to get dirty, take things apart, get involved and challenge the question as well as the answer."

Ellen Wahl
Director of Operation S M A R T.
(**S**cience **M**ath **a**nd **R**elevant **T**echnology)
Girls Clubs of America, Inc.

Today's girls need female role models who have helped advance technology. Berta Benz is a little-known example of such a woman.

If we want to remain competitive in a world economy that relies on technology, both our daughters and sons must be raised to see themselves as questioning, risk-taking individuals who strive to meet the scientific challenges before us.

Yet today:

70% of the female students in secondary vocational schools are enrolled in programs leading to traditional female jobs (clerical work, cosmetology, home economics, nursing, etc.).

Less than 10% of the skilled crafts and kindred workers are women.

In computer programming classes, boys outnumber girls nearly two to one.

Of the 21,000 members of the American Mathematical Society, only 15% are women.

Young women who do enter traditionally male fields significantly enhance their earning prospects. And with higher earning power they are much more likely to be able to support their family on their income alone, if the need arises.

But without competency in math and technology, young women cut themselves off from many of the highest paying, more rewarding careers. They limit their options at an extremely early age: Unless they take four years of high school math, they are not even eligible to major in two-thirds of all college programs.

Yet society continues to give girls subtle and not so subtle messages:

A mother who shies away from balancing the family checkbook or learning to service the car becomes a role model for her daughter.

Parents are three times more likely to send their sons to computer camp than to send their daughters.

The media portrays males holding almost all roles in technological and highly skilled fields.

What can you do to help reverse these trends?

- **If you have children of both sexes, don't expect less from your daughter than you do from your son in math and science studies.**

- **Mothers should be as involved in choosing and using a computer as fathers.**

- **Try to see that children of both sexes have equal opportunities for math and science success in the classroom. Do they get equal time on the computers?**

- **Point out women in your community who are working in nontraditional technological careers.**

- **Answer questions with questions. Become a co-learner with your child and help guide self-discovery.**

- **Encourage your daughters to learn how things are put together and how they work. Give toddlers blocks and preschoolers simple tools. Teach bicycle repair to the elementary school girl and expect the teen to put the new stereo or video tape recorder together when it arrives.**

- **Encourage exploration and risk-taking in your daughters. Let them wrestle with uncertainty and learn to analyze both failures and successes.**

As Berta Benz discovered, there's a solution to every problem, an opportunity in every failure and a car load of adventure along the way.

For more information on Operation SMART, contact Ellen Wahl, Girls Clubs of America, Inc., 30 East 33rd St. 7th Floor, New York, NY 10016.

Mindy Bingham

As co-author of the best sellers, *Choices: A Teen Woman's Journal for Self-awareness and Personal Planning,* and *Challenges: A Young Man's Journal for Self-awareness and Personal Planning,* with sales of over 400,000 to date, Mindy Bingham's interest in equity issues for girls motivates her writing. She is also co-author of *Is There A Book Inside You?* a Writer's Digest Book Club main selection, *Minou, My Way Sally, More Choices: A Strategic Planning Guide for Mixing Career and Family,* and *Changes: A Woman's Journal for Self-awareness and Personal Planning.* Mindy, a native Californian, was executive director of the Girls Club of Santa Barbara for 15 years. She has a daughter, Wendy.

Itoko Maeno

Itoko Maeno was born in Tokyo, Japan where she received her Bachelor's degree in Graphic Design. Since she came to the United States in 1982, she has focused on illustration, and her work has appeared in many books, including *Minou,* written by Mindy Bingham. Before Itoko started illustrating *Berta Benz and the Motorwagen,* she spent a week in Germany studying the countryside and visiting the Daimler-Benz Museum in Stuttgart. All technical aspects of the illustrations were carefully researched for accuracy. Car buffs and historians will enjoy this work as well as children.

Other books by Advocacy Press

You can find these books at better bookstores. Or you may send for a free catalog from Advocacy Press, P.O. Box 236, Santa Barbara, California 93102

Minou, written by Mindy Bingham, illustrated by Itoko Maeno. Hardcover with dust jacket, 64 pages with full color illustrations throughout. ISBN 0-911655-36-0.

My Way Sally, by Mindy Bingham and Penelope Paine, illustrated by Itoko Maeno. Hardcover with dust jacket, 48 pages with full color illustrations throughout. ISBN 0-911655-27-1.

Father Gander Nursery Rhymes: The Equal Rhymes Amendment, by Father Gander. Hardcover with dust jacket, full color illustrations throughout, 48 pages. ISBN 0-911655-12-3.

Tonia the Tree, by Sandy Stryker, illustrations by Itoko Maeno. Hardcover with dust jacket, 32 pages with full color illustrations throughout. ISBN 0-911655-16-6.

Kylie's Song, by Patty Sheehan, illustrated by Itoko Maeno. Hardcover with dust jacket, 32 pages with full color illustrations throughout. ISBN 0-911655-19-0.

Choices: A Teen Woman's Journal for Self-awareness and Personal Planning, by Mindy Bingham, Judy Edmondson and Sandy Stryker. Softcover, 240 pages. ISBN 0-911655-22-0.

Challenges: A Young Man's Journal for Self-awareness and Personal Planning, by Bingham, Edmondson and Stryker. Softcover, 240 pages. ISBN 0-911655-24-7.

More Choices, A Strategic Planning Guide for Mixing Career and Family, by Mindy Bingham and Sandy Stryker. Softcover, 240 pages. ISBN 0-911655-28-X.

Changes: A Woman's Journal for Self-awareness and Personal Planning, by Mindy Bingham, Sandy Stryker and Judy Edmondson. Softcover, 240 pages. ISBN 0-911655-40-9.

Mother-Daughter Choices: A Handbook for the Coordinator, by Mindy Bingham, Lari Quinn and William Sheehan. Softcover, 144 pages. ISBN 0-911655-44-1.